Passenger Flight

Passenger Flight

Brian Campbell

Carolyn Marie Souaid, Editor

Signature Editions

Cover design by Doowah Design.
Photo of Brian Campbell by Jacques Bernier.

This book was printed on Ancient Forest Friendly paper.
Printed and bound in Canada by Marquis Book Printing Inc.

We acknowledge the support of The Canada Council for the Arts and the Manitoba Arts Council for our publishing program.

Library and Archives Canada Cataloguing in Publication

Campbell, Brian
Passenger flight / Brian Campbell.

Poems.
ISBN 978-1-897109-33-5

I. Title.

PS8555.A5273 P38 2009 C811'.54 C2009-901467-X

Signature Editions
P.O. Box 206, RPO Corydon, Winnipeg, Manitoba, R3M 3S7
www.signature-editions.com

for J.

— J'aime les nuages… les nuages qui passent… là bas… là bas… les merveilleux nuages!

—Charles Baudelaire
Petits Poèmes en prose (Le Spleen de Paris)

Contents

I Sphere

II Fix

III Caesura

IV Metropolis

V Unpainted Corners

VI Flight

VII Circle

I

Sphere

Spoils

I sit on my aluminum throne. This spruce and eucalyptus-veneer table was shipped especially from Malaysia. These teak-stained tablemats, Sri Lanka. On that ersatz cherrywood shelf (Bengal), dates from Iran, mandarins from Morocco, Gala apples from Chile. This neoprene book in which I draft is from Mexico; the power cord, straight from China. The robe I wear is from Taiwan.

I am the Emperor. As I cross my kitchen (five steps) to lie on my Swedish bed, I hear the murmur of voices around my head. Such gentle hands, the servants that bear me aloft! I have every reason to trust them. But I have my spies, my plants. And now I'm told of whispered connivery: plans to poison, surprise me with a dagger, a well-timed bomb.

Poison, dagger, bomb: they have been planning it night and day, for decades. They meet via satellite, speak to each other through networks in the sky. They wear fezzes, turbans, polyester neckties. They pray to the One True God. I have never seen the One True God, although I have looked everywhere, in my closets, in my drawers, among my genitals, beneath my toenails. I am told my sin is grave. They plan infernos for every single portal of my world.

But: I am the Emperor. I sit on my plastic throne. In this nine-by-eleven-foot kitchen, I am surrounded by a collection of clocks. Every day, new clocks come in the mail, direct from Pakistan, Viet Nam, Yemen, Venezuela. Invariably they say thirty-two seconds to … is it noon, or midnight? Invariably, I wind them back, synchronize them with the others. Clocks are crucial. Clocks are indispensable. I am the Emperor of Time: I control it from this Indonesian table, this German throne.

Sphere

The sky covered by a layer of cloud. A strip of golden light: it reminds me I live on a planet. This city: rusts and coral at the bottom of a sea. There are traces of many other existences on the street, although the street is empty. Hard to believe: so many lives, just like mine. So many livers. So many lungs. So many hearts. Together we make a kind of design, although I can't perceive its form, nor the vast intricacy of its interconnections. I just go on blindly, leaving whiffs—fumes—cigarette butts—candy wrappers—infrared lines. Hi there. You are a separate life. You also leave a trail. You write in invisible ink. This ink will disappear. Each of us a photoreceptor in one colossal eye: together, we are a field of gems on the vitreous body's ocean floor. And you up there, you up there—are you? Or are you here, tracing these lines? I imagine you are you, but you are me. And this is it.

Glimpse

Rivers, stars, flowers, eyes. They peer out at me. They glint. Buttercups in grass. Orchids, great loopy filaments round pistil and stamen. Rose, concentric swirl. Sun, one of a billion billion suns. Your eyes, widening with recognition. Your eyes. All flowing into a peacock's tail, spotted whirl and flare through blackness void light-swallowing birth hole.

Whisper

Between ramparts brute and sheer, flowing water. Within that shimmering, you are there. You. Your body prone, softly breathing. What are you dreaming? Your naked form is a floating ghost. Now it vanishes. As I, too, will vanish. Shall I call you "Passage"? You pass through me, as I pass through you, within the lapping of this aqueous embrace. Who are we?

Jeunesse

Lively eyes, smooth skins, witticisms. Easy music that penetrates so deep. Prefab thoughts entirely original. I am a very sensitive instrument. Witticisms like: "I say something funny, and I get a serious answer"—these do not pass immediately into forgetfulness, but remain in the air, semi-permanent exhibits of my intelligence. We hang her canvas on the restaurant wall—harsh, brilliant, her strokes define *raw potential*, her smooth arms and flawless smile convey that potential so I really have no choice but to hold the frame while she drives in the nail. The future: a vast, unsullied savannah like the moon. So many exotic itineraries. My feet have a spring in them like the curve of her waist.

Junket

The ship's bow jerks up and down as the sea heaves mountains. Nausea rises, with it an urge to jump overboard. The sea stills. Waters harden into concrete. We are sitting in an ice cream café, the crew over there at that table, the passengers, at these tables. The captain has ordered ice cream cones. Waitresses hand them out with wan smiles. Over the hum of passing cars, a couple are in earnest discussion at a table next to mine.

"Why can't you just stick to one thing? Don't you see the value of what we have?"

"I didn't mean anything by it."

"What do you mean, *you didn't mean anything*? You were talking away, talking away, ignoring me. *You didn't even acknowledge my presence.*"

"I'm sorry. How often do I have to repeat? She's your friend; I'm not even attracted to her. It's just—we had so much in common. Anyway, she's gone now."

They natter on, a pair of seagull voices over waves.

Across the street, a bobby in his high black helmet leans into the open side window of a car by the curb. "Hey, your steering wheel's on the wrong side," I hear him say. "That car's American. How did you *get* it here?" Towers of glass and steel descend from the sky. Under their cool shadow, my ice cream isn't nearly as refreshing. Those clouds look like a galleon. No, they don't. The traffic is a river where we drown.

Claire Obscure

All this shadow, shifting in nebulous darkness. I speak of you, pursing your lips to kiss, making me step down into my body to experience the surprising pleasure. There is something in me that resists your affections. Something else that wants to blend, annihilate *me*, so that *I* urges into verb. Curious, this back and forth within my skin's parenthesis. And now I see you there, the gentle slope of your shoulders, the scoop of your breasts. I will inevitably enter your softnesses, snuggle. Within me also, this describing self, this circumscribing self that stabs with a compass, etches circles, half-moons. Shouldn't moon have an irregular plural, like mooni? Odd that one is an odd number. *Even* is so complacent in its evenness, it's odd. But rounding again to a sensual knowing: there is something very conversational about blankets, the way they rumple and bunch and collapse, form hills and valleys with each toss and turn. And when you get up, the blanket slips away, unveiling you, a statue, smooth, alabaster, yet soft in the lamplight. Your body eclipses the lamplight: penumbras slide about the room. All this play of light and shadow. Now. And thousands of years ago, in a cave.

Gallimaufry

Flick flick. Chuffle chuffle. Yes. In concupiscent caverns of hermetics, abstractions condense into moist tactilities. While the tongue goes slurp, teeth go crunch, and my crotch itches, warheads are poised in Nevada, ice caps melt in the Himalayas. The point is, as Duncan put it, a poem is a garden in the field of language that goes on and on forever. It is demarked precisely to exclude, to prevent certain combinations of flowers and vegetables from tangling which would otherwise weave warps and woofs quite wildly. This poem is only so long. I have justified it so it's square. Dandelions, crabgrass, creepers: I've left them in, planted them 圃 deliberately. Bang bang beep bip tweet tring triiiiiiiiiing! Tongue slips mind chitter. Chattering timeless: I just said so. This could be Smörgåsbord, Pastiche. But I choose Gallimaufry: this one wears galoshes and loafs around. He sports earmuffs in summer. I'm sure he speaks Old French. Pastiche is a shiksa in a camisole. Smörgåsbord, a love-handled feast, a spread. Hodge podge drives a Dodge, lives in a lodge. Or, to retreat into a green shade: *Jardin, Giardino, Gartin, Сад*, 정 원, κήπος, उघान, الحديقة Scrape scrape chuffle chuffle wirrrrrr, *voila*! Lots of peat and manure in the muck. Muck luck. If you like, here's a weeder, here's a rake. And a packet of seeds you can call your own.

II

Fix

Photo Op

Screens. Lenses. Windows. Doors. Each door a window lens screen. Photo op. So too the eyes. Digital montage: webcam click click. Earthquake, hurricane, suicide bomb: another well-coiffed commentator. No, I don't like this picture, choose that one. The self a present: the Self presents: let's hear a round of applause! Manipulations, womanipulations: hard high-gloss shoes. Splashing on of paint: purple turquoise yellow ochre crimson black blue. Oh look at that green mask: this will enhance our bathroom. Curved cut glass so *artisanale*. We must buy. Surrounded by concrete walls, paved roads, traffic lights, skin is a tender image. Surfaces galore; underneath, gore.

Nude bodies stacked on the blood-spattered floor. Woman grinning, thumbs up. For these, celebrity shots on my daily bread, gamma rays in my branded booze, billions of tax dollars in my veins.

The Angel

When a man has completely surrendered—when he cries, when he whimpers, when he gets down on all fours to kiss the toe of my boot—this is the moment of apogee, for myself and for him. Sometimes, all I have to do is appear in his cell with a pair of knitting needles; sometimes the channeling of stereophonic sound (old recordings of prisoners being severely beaten) is enough. Rarely do I, personally, have to resort to truly barbaric methods. But I have been known to. Once, to extend my limits, I had a woman put in restraints, sprinkled hydrochloric acid on her face, and while she writhed, carefully scooped out her eyes with a dessert spoon (this was recorded on video); once, ever so slowly, I crushed a man's testicles in a vice. After I acquired my reputation as the Black Angel, prisoners' eyes could be seen glazing over, their faces turning pale—some even went so far as to mutter brief prayers—at the very sight of me. This has made my work much easier.

The extraction of the confession—the famed filmed "telling all" or written signed statement—is only the ostensible purpose of my sessions. Such confessions are of flimsy reliability. The real purpose is at once more subtle and all-embracing: to take a man cloaked in "dignity," "philosophy," "rationality," in all the complacencies and subterfuges civilization has conferred upon him, and slowly, systematically *strip him* to a snivelling, squealing baby, totally at mercy of circumstance. It is fascinating to see the variations upon this theme: those who heroically resist for hours before finally giving in, and those who out of cowardice cave in immediately, in a pitiful mess of pleading, sobbing, and gratuitous betrayals of friends and family. Beyond a doubt—an extravagant moment of truth: *a most telling act of self-definition*.

Nota Bene

Ah, to see you in the soft light, in that mere and sheer lingerie, to kiss your moist lips, graceful neck and breasts, to sit you down on the sofa and—

Ah, to feel your rounded fruit, your hardening points, your wet cleft, to know my rising and entering is welcome, as is our knowledge and our laughter.

To live the finger in the crevice, the tingle of that spongy rising knoll, so difficult to find amid the folds and thickets, but what a treasure, what a ruby, that once touched, once licked and rubbed gently, magically renders such moans, such cries!

How it rises, this mast of pleasure, this seed pod in an ocean of pleasure…

In it goes. With thrust and thrust, hardness enveloped in softness, in buttocks, in kisses, more cries.

This was what I was dreaming about today.

Come home early.

Nature

Today: buskering wheat in the sheaves of afternoon. Upon the surface: overarching guava trees, damp crouching ferns, sidewinding anaconda, all manner of coral fish in intimate pools. Cities: teeming, millions upon millions in their ice cube structures, meeting, mating, spawning, dying in a thousand thousand revolving doors. Myriad lagoons, mossy deeps: and now, the harvest. She spreads herself before you.

Contrivance

Through crystalline eyes we gaze out at a vastness of floating glass squares, streets of gypsum, aluminum trees, plastic spires... and we, sheltered citizens in this charted metropolis, are also largely of plastic. Our skins are rubberized; our nervous systems, the latest polyanilines; our identities enhanced by strategically implanted microchips. We are free: free to contemplate the flickering scene through filters of anger, contentment, sorrow or hysteria. Buildings whose knife-edges cut deeply may make us cry out; or delight in the sparkle, in the thrill of abstract design. Upon chemical tides and magically generated vapours, our ship careers through space. If we smile, a mask smiles back at us, in comfort.

Fix

The global body breaks into sweats: the thermometer mounts perceptibly. But to a certain black stuff we're hooked, a black stuff that runs out. We search for it beneath mountains oceans glaciers mounds of bristling guns. We suck it up through pipes   rockets missiles jets racing cars skyscrapers tunnels underground. We rev our engines over freeway blacktop. We want and we're desperate. With twitching hands we fisticuff, bust noses, slash lips. And with syringes, stab the globe's crusty skin: how we yearn for that black gold fix in our veins.

III

Caesura

Fixate

Rear-views iced, opaque. Can only see the glows of approaching, passing strobes. I stick to my lane, afraid to change, in case a fatal brunt bears down. In the maelstrom ahead, two beady flames: little choice but follow them into the gloom.

Hyperborean

White winter silence: fog fingers curl out of my mouth. My tropical skin denies this cold: between lips and sphincter, a sac of toadstools, rose mallows, eels, tubers in mud. I fan the flames, stoke up fires. I keep it all steaming under a cover of fur.

Caesura

Waters purl, silky over smooth stones. A far-flung echo curves out among undiscovered inlets. A contour of round sound flows from mouth, forming a long bubble that snaps off and floats away on the wind. Dandelion gone to seed, seeds leaping from the porous sphere. Landscape of a horse's back and haunches. Moon setting over dunes. Wisps of air through lips of a monk as he opens the shrine. Breath humid round the folded slip of paper in his mouth. Stillness of plants. Through a microscope, tines and barbs of a feather: but still a feather, floating, tipping in air.

Perseids

The shooting stars are sky chimes in the night. We point at them and shout. Perhaps we should call them hooting stars when we shout at them. On our backs on the damp grass—two children and three adults by the lap lap lakewater—we look up. Electric messages from the infinite: little blinkings: here I am! no, I'm not! As we lie on this earth that will eventually surround us, shooting stars make ruler-lines across the sky. They flicker and fade through night's chandelier. To think: today we slumped, rolled, laughed or raced about in a voluminous present; all the while, this luminous past winked. Each of those points: a boundless vastness of gaseous eruption, flame and cloud, blue, mauve, white, roseate. Here, bring over a blanket, the night air is getting cold. Ignore the dull roar of those distant boat engines, the classic rock pounding over the water. Look, *étoile filante!*

Musika de Esferas

wisteria weaves filigree CRASH! dune shifts under still moon SMASH! sleepers turn in susurrus GASH!

GNASH! DASH! SLASH! TRASH!

BASH!

PLASH!

ASH!

IV

Metropolis

Friends

New York Jack strides over Wall Street's skyscraper canyons, cups the Guggenheim to his ear and listens to its conch-like whispers, leaps over Central Park's green rectangle, pees in Ground Zero.

Vancouver Victor swaggers down the Rockies, kicks all the sand off Wreck and Kitsilano Beaches, out-jabbers Chinatown, out-gallivants Gastown.

Toronto Tina moves those high buildings around like chess pieces. Her Queen is the CN Tower. Her shopping bag, bigger than Holt Renfrew on Bloor Street. At times, she wraps herself in the trees of High Park and slumbers.

Sydney Stephanie rolls around the Circular Quay, bounds Bondi Beach, spans Darling Harbour with her smile, reclines upon the Opera House as on a pillow.

Montreal Michel mounts Mont Royal. Served by every waitress on Duluth, Prince Arthur, and St-Denis (all at once), he out-spirals the spiral balconies, out-Oms the Big O.

When they get together, when they e-mail or even think of each other, they momentarily forget they are grains of rice in a field of rice, white dwarfs in a galaxy of exploding suns.

Systolic: 167

Blood bangs through tubes, blasts in the ears; garrotte round the forehead, vice round the heart. Sluice gates open: onrushing tidal wave of scarlet ocean. Skin oozes. I bend, shiver. Far off, a tiny pin screams.

Casements

(after Charles Baudelaire)

Through this doubled pane, the city spreads. Strings of lights delineate throughways. Pinpoints shunt the length of them. Constellations of fixed lights—an electronic Milky Way—wink in a haze of automobile fumes, steam rising from the river, dust filtering out through industrial chimneys.

Looking around my neighbourhood in these so-called wee hours, I see rectangles of variously shaded yellow or blue light suspended among the shadows. Across the street, framed in a silhouette of century-old moulding, I see under a single incandescent bulb a row of kitchen cabinets. Occasionally a hand reaches up, opens a cupboard, takes down a bottle of whiskey from several others on the shelf. The hand is gnarled, age-spotted—man or woman I cannot tell for sure. Several other rectangles glow with a bluish, spectral hue: I imagine other solitudes crouching over computer screens, sending digital self-portraits around the world.

Across the ocean of roofs, I see a middle-aged woman, her face already lined, who rarely if ever goes out. Often, as now, she slouches motionless in front of a television. I can only imagine her frown: out of that imaginary frown, out of practically nothing at all I have made up this woman's story, or rather legend, and sometimes I tell it to myself and my eyes water; but I do not weep. Perhaps my compassion—could this be called compassion?—is anesthetized by her own ceaseless foray into distraction. Perhaps in one of these casements, someone is observing my square—dimly illuminated by this screen on which I write—and thinking: there is an oblivious one, a little life, unaware of all others! Yet imagining these lives, even the one observing mine—hasn't it helped me to see my own, to feel that I am what I am—but one open eye among the many eyes of the city?

There She Lies

There she lies, carefree hair, airbrushed shoulders on his weight-machined pecs: bottom right RALPH LAUREN ROMANCE. There she stands, empty hall, eyes closed, kimono open: flush left MISSONI. There she struts, cobblestone street, stiletto-heeled, tight black leather: across the top VERSACE. There she gazes, eyes of doe, vanilla skin, waxy lips: spread wide below MAYBELLINE.

Minotaur

Walls, fences, corridors; some clammy, wet, carved out of earth; others of stainless steel; still others spiky, embedded with broken glass. Fear mounts as I near each blind corner: what's on the other side? Word has it of a beast with the body of a bull, the eyes and forehead of a man, and a long trap-like jaw of serrated teeth. Who eats humans alive. Whose breath stinks of carrion. I myself have never heard even an echo of his roar: all this could be fantastic rumour. For there are thousands here with me, all around me, backs hunched, picking their way through parallel hallways; sometimes I see them, most of the time I am alone. Once I came upon a cavern, where hundreds had gathered. "We should build a grand tunnel," one proclaimed from a podium, "so we can all go together!"—his remarks greeted by shouts and applause. But another countered from another podium: "No! We have to develop our sniffer-dog instincts—find our *own* way through the way!" More pandemonium. As for me, I have designed my own light which I strap to my helmet. It makes me, if not proud, reconciled to my groping path. Presently, barely visible in the darkness, looms a series of guard towers shaped like helmets, slits in their visors. Rows of turrets and buttresses webbed with barbed wire. I feel my way beneath them. In dark corners and under bushes, what look like clutches of people. I catch snatches of their whispers: "… mount together… crushed… pummeled… aren't they trying to get across … no, we want to go *there!*" Maybe I will find my own rainbow, and beyond that, gold. That's what they tell us: rainbow, gold.

Arena

Keening sand rasps rocks round. Ocean's rough wet tongue bores holes through bluffs. Red walls fade pink, whiten in the sun. Cracks: brown streaks: rusty pipe. Ancient typewriter, keys jammed, tossed out on the beach. Hub and gears that once turned smoothly now go squeak squeak. And a city falls into itself, roofs upon foundations.

Petal withers, drifts
to the floor.

Tap drips,
washers rubbing thin.

My skin creased,
worn

to blanched

bone.

Unpainted Corners

Bathyscaphe

Under a scalloped blue ceiling, gilled ellipses. Tentacled spheres and bulge-eyed cylinders tumble and swirl. Needle jaws snap over transparent lives, which in turn have snapped, severed, swallowed. Silver darts glide upward, cleave through the ceiling, slice back in again. For the largest of them and for me, there is a visible ceiling, a distant floor. But for the tiniest, blackness in all directions. As when I close my eyes, I become blackness in all directions: a molecular it.

Slough

Everything under a thin skin of dust. In the stillness it falls like snow. Beautiful, this falling. Soon I will be a part of it: accumulate on other bodies; as they move, they'll shed my presence. We are all shedding presences of the dead. I shake a glass globe: a flaked storm whirls and settles. Shake again: multitudes in feathery whiteness. Galaxies are inhaled and exhaled with every breath.

Conte

"Once upon a time," he said.

"Once... upon... a... time..."

"Once."

Why once? Why just once, among at least two hundred billion humans living or dead, sixty-five hundred quadrillion organisms, one thousand decillion octogintillion septuagintillion to the power of googolplexplexplexplexplexplexplex of stars, gas giants, comets, meteors and cold clumps of earth? Why once?

"Upon."

Upon a time. How upon? A time, especially a time? How can anyone be upon a time? Why not within? Without? Inside? Out? Under, over, in front of, in back of, beside, above, beyond?

"Twice beneath a time."

"Thrice beyond a time."

"One hundred thousand three hundred and forty-six nonagintillion duocentillion sextendecillion times without..."

...a time? Why not space? Space-time time-space space-time times time-space?

Why *a?* Why not *the?* Why not beyond above beneath in back of in front of *a* or *the?* Why not *between* a and the?

"Thrice throughout the spaces, two dwarfs and a bear..."

"Forty-nine times within outside a space-time discontinuum, this raven-eyed witch..."

"In a nonillion of spaces contained within each other, beyond all time, beyond all space, here now but not now ever, there was this golden-haired girl..."

"Ninety times twice times thrice at least, this time and last time, within a moctogentillion googolplexplexplexplexplexplex of non-times and non-spaces repeated over and over within time/space multiplied indefinitely inside a realm of unrepeatable nothing/something void/ fullness, there was—will be—this man, woman, shall we say character, this non-person personage, who cannot ever be or say or even pronounce without everlasting transient strangeness

once

upon

a

time

.

"

My Oh-So-Friendly Alter Ego

His modesty made me think of broken columns
    his smile   of crumbling stone fences

"There is a people," he said, "a desert, tribal people, who when they paint their houses leave a corner unpainted, so as not to rival the perfection of God. Think of my

[omissions]

as my unpainted corners."

His heart was a cavern. But it was cozy in there: there were spiderwebs,
and bugs, and rotting mattresses, and easy chairs, and books, and
ancient
    yellow
photographs

Self-Portrait #253

Face pressed against a windowpane, nose and fingers flat as undersides of snails. Breath misting up the glass: the whole head becomes a globe in fog.

Zog

Log. Bog. Mulch of larch, mulberry leaves. Slime-wet stone soil, twisting, tangly root hair. Fungus ratatouille. Scrunch scrunch: silkworms patter over the mesentery. And curving upwards, strung with water beads: stem, calyx, blossom bell. Croaking frogs a cattail chorus: *Zog. Zog.*

Precambrian

Out of tectonic torsion, mountains surge; in deep earthen fissures, a glacier seeps and gurgles. Sky an ashen monochrome. Here, emotion is a quivering insect, a twisting blues amid rock and ice. Out of the silence, a grinding motion; crevasses open; fingers of mud rush downward, plug holes in silt layers, petrify. Mushroom grows blindly in the dark.

Flight

Conspiracy

In China, thousands upon thousands of assembly lines crank out the cubes, tubes and dunce caps of our every want and need. In India, electronic lotuses bloom from ghostly interface schematics. The Cyber Sutra is being written, inscribed into our souls. All this in accordance with the Revised Grandmaster Marketing Plan drawn up in Riyadh and Chattanooga.

We hold hands. We walk on a sidewalk in a metropolis. Our words to each other are wisps; our kiss, a vanishing point. We feel and say, "We are nothing." Yet we are quite certain all this vast hypnosis dangles from the watch chain of our kiss.

Airport

(after Charles Baudelaire)

So we were up all night getting plastered, then two hours at the airport bar. When I saw him off, I was so bummed I didn't know where the fuck to go. So I wandered—stood in the waiting area, don't know how long. Gazed at the sky, at the mobile clouds. Looked across at the velvety runways going in all directions, at the flashing lights. Suddenly I was inside this prism of oddity. The airships, gliding in and taking flight, revived a taste for rhythm and beauty. No need to dwell on the marvel of all those tonnes borne aloft: but the marvel remained, leaving me faint, light-headed as that thinnest air, kilometres above the ground. And because I no longer had even an ounce of ambition, for hours I took a mysterious, aristocratic pleasure in watching, as I leaned over a handrail in the mezzanine, all the bustle of people leaving, of people returning, people who still have enough energy to have desires, who still desire to voyage, to get rich.

Passport

It began in Amsterdam, the women peering from black-lighted windows. I took one for my own. Her name was Chantalina: long-limbed, blonde—real centrefold. And what a way with her tongue! I grew to love her accent.

In Istanbul, her name was Tatiana. She was from Kiev. She had sad eyes. But such a slender thing! I loved to make her smile. When she told me of her son, born with tumours in his throat, she rocked in my arms and cried. She was sold.

In Bangkok, I lived up to the city's name. I had as many as three in my bed. We played the *sueng* on the sound system as we had sex—I like to feel indigenous in a place like that. Once I had two of them come together, then I came too. That old Kama Sutra comes in handy! They were my size: they looked up to me when we walked the streets. (Good things come in small packages.) I look forward to their silken skins, their tiny hands.

In Dubai, I had a house beneath the sea. A belly dancer danced for me amid the sharks and whales. Her name was Amarantha—the first truly buxom woman to make me feel alive.

By then, I had arranged my affairs around these affairs.

I moved my factories from zone to zone, through hemispheres.

I added specialties: shoes, bracelets, Christmas figurines. Then guns.

I purchased my own jet.

In French Polynesia I couldn't resist a tattoo. One tattoo makes you itch for another, then another: on my upper arm, my shoulder blade, down my back. I got them on return trips. Dragons embedded with initials of my lovers, they're like passport pages on my skin. They make me mysterious at parties. "*You*—a tattoo? Can we see it?" "It's too far back. Maybe another time."

Soon my wife disappeared into others' arms. She was a bad investment from the start. Couldn't keep up with changing times! I send our children postcards—sometimes from Shanghai, sometimes from Mumbai, once from Baffin Island. I'm a responsible Pop. They say I'm *just awesome*. And they have nothing to worry about: I have a hefty trust fund set aside, just for their education.

Field of Gems

Out into blue-white spaces, a field of crystals and gems: pearl, onyx, sapphire, lapis lazuli. The stars hang, pear-shaped opals. The planets are polished moonstones, sunstones. I gaze at them from within my sockets. Bells reverberate, resound in rain, wrap the landscape in silver strands. I am a pupa in this shining cocoon. I am wrapped by one silver strand.

Eyes

Eyes peer in at me, in dreams, in crowds. Eyes look up from desks, around edges of partitions. Eyes bear down on me, in corridors, washrooms, department stores, subway tunnels. Electronic eyes in walls record my every movement. Camera eyes track my vehicle, issue tickets in my name. At the border, a lens records my iris; another images my voice. I pay for this: a surtax, to keep me safe. How did I, supernumerary, become so important? But in my insignificance is danger: they imagine I seethe in fury, have live ammo strapped to me, readied to explode. And indeed, tucked within me like a dagger, I do have that fury: I too am a digital camera, recording their transgressions. Even as I type, at midnight, in this cottage in the country: scuffle, scratch: a masked face, cloaked spy at the window. Hey! I shout. *Raccoon.*

Behind the Eyelids

Behind the eyelids are layers of paisley, a shifting, breathing Persian carpet. Rectangles form, spread, dissolve. Rows of granules become spuming waves, meshes that sway in an ocean current. Networks of veins, patterns of leaves. Now crepuscular darkness brightens to orange, becomes sun behind fog: I grope through a room, touch a warm lampshade; slide my hand along a wall.

When The Music Is Not On I Hear

whirr of air conditioner fans, clack of refrigerator doors, water-swash pot lid tap-tap-tap. Voices mingle in the echo. A pen drops; keyboards whisper. Two waiters: *6:00, isn't it?... yeah, that's when Marie takes over.* All part of the rumble that tumbles on beyond all books

Passenger Flight

On my return flight from anywhere to nowhere, because I have ordered the tickets late, the agent tells me there is only one seat left. The proviso is that I will have to sit beside a man who was badly burned in a war. "Do you mind?" she asks. I reply, with some reluctance, "I suppose not." I really have to take my flight today.

As usual I am one of the last passengers: almost everyone has already taken their seat. I find and take mine. The seat beside me is empty. Inwardly, I rejoice: maybe the man has canceled his flight. From the seat pocket in front of me, I pull out *High Life* magazine: on the cover, a smiling model, her shiny blonde hair and glossy complexion photoshopped to perfection. Behind it is the laminated card with safety procedures. I unfold it: there is our plane, in perfect condition, floating on evenly tipped navy-blue waves, yellow inflatable ramps extending down from the exit doors. People slide down in red life jackets. It looks like fun. At that moment, I feel a shadowy presence lower itself beside me. Out of the side of my eye, I see a trench coat and fedora tipped forward over dark glasses. I turn to look: not only is the man's face mottled and burned, but part of his cheek eaten away so one can see his yellowing teeth back to the molars. Spit dribbles over a pustule-covered jaw. An odour emanates: formaldehyde. He turns, says as casually as he can, "Hi." He asks me where I am flying. I tell him, simply, home. He tells me he is also flying from "back there" (pointing a bony thumb towards the back of the plane) to St. Kitts, where he is from. When he says "St. Kitts," spittle flies on my lap and the back of the next seat. In St. Kitts (spit, spit), everyone knows him, so he can be accepted, somewhat. Back there everyone was anonymous, so he was unable to make friends with anyone. It was so lonely. Presently we fall silent. What can I say to him? Ask him about his burns? But he speaks in a monotone, as if by rote, as if everything he says has been repeated too many times before. Something in me wants to pursue the conversation, as if to prove to myself what a good, tolerant man I am.

"At least it's sunny," I say, pointing to the blue Plexiglas oval beside us. "The view should be fantastic."

"For those who have one," he says. I realize he would have to crane.

"It must be hard to get to know people," I say, trying to wring sympathy out of dry vocal cords.

"I take to people," he says. "You might even call me a 'people person.'" More spit spatters the back of the next seat. "But they have trouble taking to me."

Silence falls over us again. Now I truly don't know what to say. He shifts, turns away. Clearly, he feels my unease. Others around us try to ignore him, chat about inconsequential things. A movie flickers on the overhead television screens: canned laughter squeaks out through hundreds of earphones. But sitting here, I prefer our shared silence. Eventually, perhaps, I will get used to him.

VII

Circle

Death

White frame house, freshly painted, on a gentle hill. Windowless, save for a little room up top—two tiny round portholes, drapes closed, like shut eyes. Around the house, yellow grass. No trees, no neighbours. We are standing in front. "This is our house." These words come as a thought, not from you, not from me. It is understood that here is where we will spend our lives. We go inside, me leading the way. In the darkness, ornate heirloom furniture, heavy grandmothery armchairs and sofas with doilies on their backs. The air is musty, suffocating. We need to get out—fast.

We are outside. The sunlight is brilliant. The house is blinding white, too white to look at. All around, an empty yellow plain, leading to a flat, featureless horizon. We have set up a table. On it we have gathered things remaining from our previous life—file folders, candles, pots, a few odd mugs, two broken pencils, a clock with no hands. We intend it as a garage sale. But it is clear that no one will come to buy.

Edmonton

Vast flatness an empty stage for tormenting clouds, bunching storms. Skeletal requirements of an abstract landscape: land and sky: you can draw the line with a ruler. The streets are ruled too—87th Street 86th Street 85th Street 102nd Avenue. Even the buildings: scalpel edges: Home Depot The Running Room A&W IGA BCBG Banana Republic Costco The Brick Fairweather Dollarama Zellers Dairy Queen Taco Bell Pizza Hut McDonald's. Poetry is compared to the filling of potholes here and found wanting. All new money: the coins for change all shiny. The Sikh at the 7-Eleven, the Yoruba at Wal-Mart, the Jamaican cleaning lady at Journey's End, are pressed into service. Potholes are made even with the horizon line: no jolts.

Pastorale

Westerlies hum through tall, pale grass. Highway murmurs in the distance. Crimson barn. Gabled farmhouse. High fence, topped with electric wire.

Restricted Area
WARNING

Meadowlark wheels, alights on a tree branch.

Holsteins low, chuff at their troughs.

Silos beyond that fence point downward. Minutemen, in their gleaming white coats, stand at attention. Titanium cones point upward.

PHOTOGRAPHING, MAKING NOTES, DRAWINGS, MAPS, OR GRAPHIC REPRESENTATION OF THIS AREA OR ITS ACTIVITIES IS PROHIBITED

Alert Status

Green	Blue	Yellow	Orange	Red
ON DECK	SELECTED	READY	TRACK	FIRE

Quality Control

Knife plunges into the cow's oesophagus, blood splashes over gowns: stacks of boxes on a stockroom floor. Lines of my name in a telephone directory: Campbell Brian 264 Dalhousie St. 514-555-6568 Campbell Brian 372 Delaware St. 514-etc. Rows of identical houses bracket each other up graded hills. Cars blur past under traffic lights stop go stop go stop go. Banks of URLs in the spammer's outbox Select All Control C Control V Press Delete. Copper wires tunnel through green fields of motherboard.
These parallel lines draw together in a distance.
I is a vanishing point.

Reversal of Fortune

Ground and sky have exchanged positions: change falls out of my pockets into the blue expanse below. Like great birds, newspapers curl, unfurl as they blow across the pavement. Everything is deserted: cars rest on their roofs, wheels in the air. I walk the median, one foot in front of the other on the yellow paint, lest I plunge into asphalt depths.

Hungry, I look up. A restaurant:

KNOW LUCK CHINESE AND CANADIAN FOOD

I have always wanted to know what Canadian food was like. Pizza? French fries? I step inside.

The restaurant, too, is empty—Arborite tables, chrome chairs—but for one gangly Oriental waiter, menus in arm, his blank face betraying a slight trace of bewilderment.

"Could I have some Canadian food, please?" I ask.

"I'm sorry, we're all out. All we have left are misfortune cookies."

Before me he places a plate: pockets of cardboardy sweetness. I look out the window: the street has disappeared. Our restaurant floats on cauliflower clouds. I crack open the beige shells one by one, pull out the pink-lettered strips:

DON'T KID YOURSELF: YOU ARE UNLOVEABLE.

GIVE UP WHILE YOU'RE AHEAD.

ALL YOUR DREAMS WILL COME TRUE—AND BECOME YOUR WORST NIGHTMARES.

SOON YOU WILL DIE—AND BE BURIED BY A NECROPHILIAC.

Slick

Little slithery ink ball, wings stuck. Bleats from a bird throat. Low slow moan. Bodies lift, succumb to gummy plumbed crude seep. And the blot laps miles: purple green sheen.

Brainpan

The day is a creased grey brain. Leaves, like scuttling claws, scrape and eddy across the streets. Wind howls through a funnel of nightmare. Leather collars are turned up against the cold. Now rivulets flow into gutters, flooding damp earth: green shoots sprout despite the coming winter. The trees hide sap within their gnarled coats. Smudged, bent figures in the rain are pedestrians walking head down, engraving the sidewalk's grooves deep into their cerebrums. But beyond the brooding masses in the sky—canyons of light, brilliant rays under a blinding white disc.

Concentric

In my box within a box within a box—kitchen, apartment, building complex—I look around at roundnesses: vases, flowers, bottles, plates, clementines in a bowl. Candle, concentric craters round the wick. Tapers of arms, thighs. Your face, my face: circles. Movement of free hand: circles. Oval of sky, corona of sun, blue-bubble planet, dust ring swirl. Why inhabit these boxes within boxes? Why await a long wooden rectangle to carry us into the next round world?

Wacky Woo

Wacky woo. But really woo. Waltz together to Javanese gongs, ululate an uvular song. Somersault in scuba fins, go slappity slap round the Dead Sea's rim. Sprinkle the last snows of Tahiti over each other like confetti. Sing "Here Comes The Bride" in Kazakh and Kradai; make them entirely harmonize. Carry her upstairs under a lintel; lay her down in a chamber—entirely of rose petals. Order burgers, fries, and chocolate-covered apples; devour them by candlelight. Massage each other with Velcro—but warmly, gently, so your skins just glow. Make a spell: circle her thrice, ring a bell, swing a cut lily over your heads, chant Ding Dong Dell.

Flounce

Flurries into deep fluff: flossy the fleece of fleurs-de-lys. Flimflams flagellate, but soon fluster. Flammable flannelmouths flog flummery; we flout with flare, unflappable. Fledgeling flinders fling and fly. Fliff, flaff; flimsy this fluttery flume. But flexuous. And now we flaunt forth, unfurl with flourish our flashing flambeau.

Speechify

Stentorian *elocutio*—man on a podium waving his arms—hey, that's me. I rhetoricize through funnels, epoxidized circuit boards. Skeins of black cable burst through my mouth. And amidst this amplified blast and crackle: a fugitive whisper: myself to myself: *this not real, this not really this*. Maybe all this is megalithic grandstanding, an *über alles* of verbal pyrotechnic. Ghosting beneath, a ripple on water: breath between breaths. Air

To A Writer Who Complains

Cut yourself free from all telecommunications: fax phone email radio TV Internet DAP SMS. Live alone in your room, which you have emptied of all but a writing desk, a chair, a pile of blank paper, a pen or pencil, and yourself. Locate that room several hundred miles underground or up in the air. Block its door with strips of zinc hammered to the jambs; its windows with sheets of iron. Now revel in the silence. The mind fills a void. It does fill. Have faith.

Fishy

The poetry editor of a magazine to which I had recently submitted sent me an e-mail asking permission not to print my poems, but to kindly let him grind them up into fish food. "In our aquarium," he explained, "we have several exotic fish, and we are of the opinion that your poems, ground up, would make an ideal nutrient for them." "Will you eventually publish them?" I wrote back. "No, we're afraid your poems, however worthy they may be, do not meet our editorial needs at this time." "Will I be able to publish them elsewhere?" was my next question. "Only," he replied, "if the publisher agrees to print them with this credit underneath: —*Originally ground up as fish food for The Barracuda Review.* However," he added, "we also think that your poems, grated, might serve as an excellent condiment for Italian food. If you agree, we'll try them on our Fettuccini Alfredo tonight." Reflecting on this, I realized it's true: poems don't have to be read to be appreciated. I accepted his offer, although not without feelings of regret and chagrin.

The Stillness Minnow

I cup my hands, close them around it, slowly, slowly… trying to move my fingers without moving. It darts away.

We were closer to it when we lay together, sharing breaths and whispers. We were closer when we rested in silence, caressing our privates, making them warm, engorge.

Now I in chair, you in couch, books in hand, we are clamshelled in fashion statements. And it suspends in the air between us.

Its scales are golden, with two bands of blue down its sides. Under transparent skin, a single, silver lung contracts, expands. The tiny glove of its heart beats. A luminous bubble comes from its mouth, floats up out of sight.

Blowze

drowsy blowzy, a great blouse of clouds. ethereal undulations, gaseous deeps. down there, in feathery canyons, my limbs melted. I am faint of oxygen. no birds: only flight. tufts, tawny sunlight. whorls, white. all circular, framed in this transparent bubble. and the serpents in my eyes, in my milky brain, hiss, writhe as their blood turns to vapour at this height. such a wonderful flying machine: scarcely audible the engine's purr. I have only just awoken. I hurtle past in the huge luge of my craft.

Notes

The epigraph is from the closing lines of "L'Etranger" (The Stranger), the opening prose poem in Charles Baudelaire's *Paris Spleen*. The translation by Louise Varèse reads:

> "Then, what do you love, extraordinary stranger?"
> "I love the clouds … the clouds that pass … up there …
> up there … the wonderful clouds!"

In "Gallimaufry" the foreign words and symbols are simply "garden" in various languages. The central symbol is Traditional Chinese, specifically, for public or nursery garden. In the final lines, "garden" appears in French, Italian, German, Russian, Korean, Greek, Sanskrit, and Arabic.

"Casements" and "Airport" are palimpsests of "Windows" and "Seaports" by Charles Baudelaire, as translated by Louise Varèse in *Charles Baudelaire: Paris Spleen* (New York: New Directions Books, 1970).

When I titled "Arena," I was thinking of the Spanish word "arena," which means "sand," although it also carries the English sense of "arena." "Arena" derives from the Latin *harena*, meaning variously sand, sandy place, seashore, and place of combat (literally, "place strewn with sand").

The *sueng* in "Passport" is a plucked string instrument from Northern Thailand.

"Pastorale": The language on the signs is from a Nike missile site in the San Francisco Bay area, now run as a public military museum after the missiles were decommissioned in the 1970's. An entire slide show is readily accessible by Internet. Inside the control room are rows of indicator lights used in the deployment of these weapons. These are labeled with the multicoloured Alert Status and ON DECK SELECTED READY TRACK FIRE. For the generation of Minuteman intercontinental missiles in current use, such indicators may well be an anachronism—but that, of course, I am in no position to know.

Acknowledgements

Grateful acknowledgement is made to the following publications in whose pages some of these prose poems, or versions of them, first appeared: *The New Quarterly*, *Vallum*, *Geez*, *MiPOesias*, *Montreal Serai*, *Dusie*, *Nth Position*, *Eclectica*, *Evergreen Review*, and the *2004 Cranberry Tree Press Anthology*.

A selection of these poems was shortlisted for the 2006 CBC Literary Award for Poetry.

I'd like to extend my appreciation to Allen Sutterfield, Nina Bruck, Elise Moser, and Heather Spears. Their close reading and suggestions helped make a number of these prose poems flight-worthy. Special thanks to Raphael Bendahan: our many hours of delightful poetry conversation and critiquing not only helped me streamline these poems, but contributed to some of my most vivid trajectories.

Further gratitude to Carolyn Marie Souaid and Karen Haughian at Signature Editions, for their dedication in bringing this manuscript into its final form.

And very special thanks to Jocelyne Dubois, for her unfailing love and support, and for restoring my faith that poetry—and prose poetry—matters.

The Author

Montreal-based poet, singer-songwriter, editor, and translator Brian Campbell is the author of *Guatemala and Other Poems* (1994) and *Undressing the Night* (2007), a translation of the selected poems of Nicaraguan-Canadian poet Francisco Santos. His poetry, reviews, and essays have appeared in literary magazines such as *The Antigonish Review, Vallum, CV2, The New Quarterly, Grain, Prairie Fire, Rock Salt Plum Review, The Rover,* and *The Saranac Review.* A finalist in the 2006 CBC Literary Award for Poetry, he is also the co-founder/editor of *Sky of Ink Press*, which prints quality chapbooks by emerging poets. His independent music CD, *The Courtier's Manuscript*, was released in 2002. Brian Campbell teaches English as a Second Language to adults, and does freelance translation. Visit his blog and website at www.briancampbell.org

Eco-Audit
Printing this book using Rolland Enviro 100 Print instead of virgin fibres paper saved the following resources:

Trees	Solid Waste	Water	Air Emissions	Natural Gas
3	76 kg	7,208 L	167 kg	11 m³